I0815347

DiscoverRoo
An Imprint of Pop!
popbooksonline.com

The Eras of Taylor Swift

THE SPEAK NOW era

Track List

1. Mine
2. Sparks Fly
3. Back to December
4. Speak Now
5. Dear John
6. Mean
7. The Story of Us
8. Never Grow Up
9. Enchanted
10. Better Than Revenge
11. Innocent
12. Haunted
13. Last Kiss
14. Long Live

by Elizabeth Andrews

WELCOME TO DiscoverRoo!

This book is filled with videos, puzzles, games, and more! Scan the QR codes* while you read, or visit the website below to make this book pop.

popbooksonline.com/SpeakNow

abdobooks.com

Published by Pop!, a division of ABDO, PO Box 398166, Minneapolis, Minnesota 55439.

Printed in the United States of America, North Mankato, Minnesota.

082025
012026

Cover Photo: Alexandra Tarasova (BigArtLab); Shutterstock Images

Interior Photos: AP Images; Getty Images; Shutterstock Images; Wikimedia Fandom; WENN Rights Ltd/Alamy Stock Photo; ZUMA Press, Inc./Alamy Stock Photo

Editor: Grace Hansen and Anna Schwartz

Series Designer: Laura Graphenteen

Library of Congress Control Number: 2025941228

Publisher's Cataloging-in-Publication Data

Names: Andrews, Elizabeth, author.

Title: The Speak Now era / by Elizabeth Andrews

Description: Minneapolis, Minnesota : Pop!, 2026 | Series: The eras of Taylor Swift | Includes online resources and index

Identifiers: ISBN 9781098248758 (lib. bdg.) | ISBN 9781098249274 (ebook)

Subjects: LCSH: Swift, Taylor, 1989- --Juvenile literature. | Popular music--Juvenile literature. | Popular (Songs, etc.)--Juvenile literature. | Albums--Juvenile literature. | Concerts--Juvenile literature. | Mass media and music--Juvenile literature.

Classification: DDC 782.42164100--dc23

*Scanning QR codes requires a web-enabled smart device with a QR code reader app and a camera.

TABLE OF CONTENTS

CHAPTER 1

ROUND THREE

Taylor Swift was coming off of wonderful success in the summer of 2010. Her second album, *Fearless*, won the **Grammy** for Album of the Year! This was the most respected award of the night. The world was waiting to see what she would do next.

WATCH A VIDEO HERE!

Birthday: December 13, 1989
Star Sign: Sagittarius
Place of Birth: West Reading, PA
Favorite Number: 13
Favorite Color: Purple
Favorite Meal: Chicken tenders and a chocolate shake

Meredith Grey

13

Benjamin Button

X O X O

Olivia Benson

Taylor Swift

On August 4, 2010, "Mine" hit listeners' ears. The song's release was a surprise even to Taylor and her team. It was leaked 12 days before they planned to send it out to radio stations. "Mine" was the lead **single** from Taylor Swift's third **studio** album. The music video would soon follow.

Taylor started showing fans love with heart hands on the Fearless *tour.*

Taylor first saw the male lead from the "Mine" music video in a film. She knew she wanted him in her video.

"Mine" **debuted** at number 3 on the Billboard Hot 100. It was a classic Taylor song with more mature thoughts on love. Taylor teased fans with the song's meaning in a livestream before it was released. She said she wrote the song when she saw an entire relationship flash before her eyes. It is about her pattern of running from love.

On August 27, the music video premiered. Country Music Television (CMT) hosted a live half-hour special leading up to the video release with behind-the-scenes footage of its making. The music video follows the story of young Taylor being upset by her parents' relationship. She grows up and falls in love. Viewers watch her wild relationship and eventually see Swift and the leading man get married and have children.

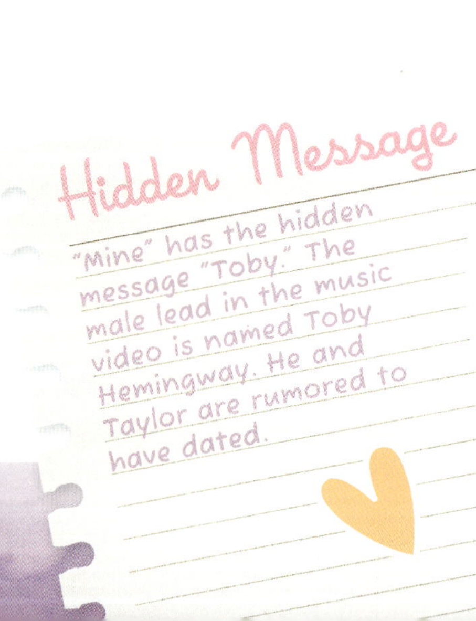

Hidden Message

"Mine" has the hidden message "Toby." The male lead in the music video is named Toby Hemingway. He and Taylor are rumored to have dated.

Taylor performed a special concert at the town in Maine where the "Mine" music video was filmed.

CHAPTER 2

SPEAK NOW

The world was waiting on Taylor Swift's third album. On October 25, 2010, it was theirs. Like Taylor's previous two albums, *Speak Now* was **produced** by Nathan Chapman and released through Big

EXPLORE LINKS HERE!

Machine Records. It **debuted** at number 1 on Billboard 200. All the songs from the album charted on the Billboard Hot 100.

Speak Now ***sold 1,047,000 copies in its first week!***

Speak Now

Taylor Swift

Speak Now faced a lot of pressure to be great after the success of *Fearless*. Luckily, the moment after her second album was released, Taylor started writing for *Speak Now*. She stated, "I love to plan 20 steps ahead." This album was the first she wrote entirely herself.

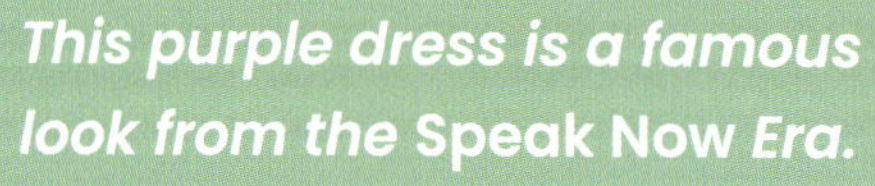

This purple dress is a famous look from the Speak Now *Era.*

Taylor and Chapman recorded most of the album in Chapman's basement **studio**. Many of the songs featured first-take vocals. Music **critics** applauded Taylor's more grown-up lyrics and stronger voice. They noticed she was using her vocal range to show the different emotions in her lyrics.

Speak Now *won the world record for fastest-selling digital album in 2010.*

Taylor Swift surprised fans in Los Angeles with a performance on a double-decker bus.

Taylor wrote a song called "Babe" during the Speak Now Era. She gave it to the band Sugarland.

Taylor was happy about the applause for her vocals. In January 2010, she had a difficult performance at the **Grammys**. Her singing was off and people gave her trouble for it. Her team defended her by saying Taylor has never been known for perfect vocals. She is known for the emotions she puts in her songs.

CHAPTER 3

BEHIND THE LYRICS

At 14 songs, some people thought *Speak Now* was too long. Swifties did not feel the same. They connected with the honest lyrics that covered everything from love and heartbreak to bullies and growing up. Taylor has stated that her songs capture certain feelings or moments many young people experience.

COMPLETE AN ACTIVITY HERE!

Taylor gave an emotional performance of "Back to December" at the 2010 American Music Awards.

Taylor Lautner was many peoples' crush in the early 2010s. He was a star of the Twilight *movie series.*

The second **single** off the album was "Back to December." Listeners guessed that the song was about Taylor Lautner. Swift met him while filming the movie *Valentine's Day*. They seemed to date for a few months and eventually break it off. The couple was never official. According to the timeline Swifties created of Taylor's dating life, December is likely the month she ended things with Lautner.

DID YOU KNOW?

Taylor Lautner has confirmed "Back to December" is about him. He is still friends with Taylor today.

The most awarded song off *Speak Now* is "Mean." It won the **Grammy** for Best Country Solo Performance and Best Country Song. "Mean" is about when someone goes from **critiquing** to attacking everything about a person. Swifties think it is likely written about a specific journalist who wrote a very mean article about Taylor's 2010 Grammys performance.

Taylor used her performance of "Mean" at the 2011 Grammys to prove her haters wrong.

"Long Live" is the final song on the album. Taylor described it as a love letter to her fans. She wrote it about her band, **producer**, and all the people who helped build her career and were a part of her successes. Fans love this song because it is about friendship and memories. It became an **anthem** for many graduating high school seniors.

Taylor Swift released a perfume called Wonderstruck inspired by the song "Enchanted."

CHAPTER 4

ENCHANTING THE WORLD

Taylor took *Speak Now* on the road with a tour that began on February 11, 2011. She sold out 110 arena concert dates across 76 countries. The stage was designed like a theater. It included fireworks, ballerinas, church bells, a giant rotating tree, and costume changes.

LEARN MORE HERE!

Speak Now World Tour made nearly $100 million!

Much of Speak Now's style was inspired by the decorations Taylor used in the first home she bought.

Speak Now (Taylor's Version) came out on July 7, 2023. Taylor dropped a lot of Easter eggs for her fans before she announced it. In the 2022 "Bejeweled" music video, instrumental versions of "Long Live" and "Enchanted" can be heard playing. At the end of the video there are castles crumbling and three dragons flying. She mentions dragons in "Long Live," and there is a vault song called "Castles Crumbling."

Taylor's koi fish guitar went missing from a museum just before Speak Now (Taylor's Version) *came out. It reappeared when Taylor played it on the Eras Tour.*

LUCKY #13

Speak Now (Taylor's Version) had another major Easter egg in the "Bejeweled" music video. Taylor enters an elevator with 13 floor button options. The buttons for 3 and 13 are both purple. Taylor presses number 3. *Speak Now* is her third album and the era's color is purple. Fans guessed that since button 13 matches, Taylor must be hinting that she was about to drop *Speak Now (Taylor's Version)*. Sure enough, that rerecording became her 13th album.

Joey King (right) was in the music video for "Mean." Taylor brought her back for the "I Can See You" music video.

The first single from *Speak Now (Taylor's Version)* is the vault song "I Can See You." The music video was written and **directed** by Taylor. In it, she is being held in a vault. None other than Taylor Lautner is on his way to save her! He runs through a museum of Taylor Swift **memorabilia**. When Taylor is released from the vault, she steals *Speak Now (Taylor's Version)* off the wall. It was a fun video for Swifties to study!

Songs "From the Vault" are tracks that Taylor recorded for the original album but didn't release. They are included on Taylor's Versions.

DID YOU KNOW?

The magazine *Rolling Stone* wrote, "Swift's third album, *Speak Now*, is roughly twice as good as 2008's *Fearless*, which was roughly twice as good as her 2006 **debut**."

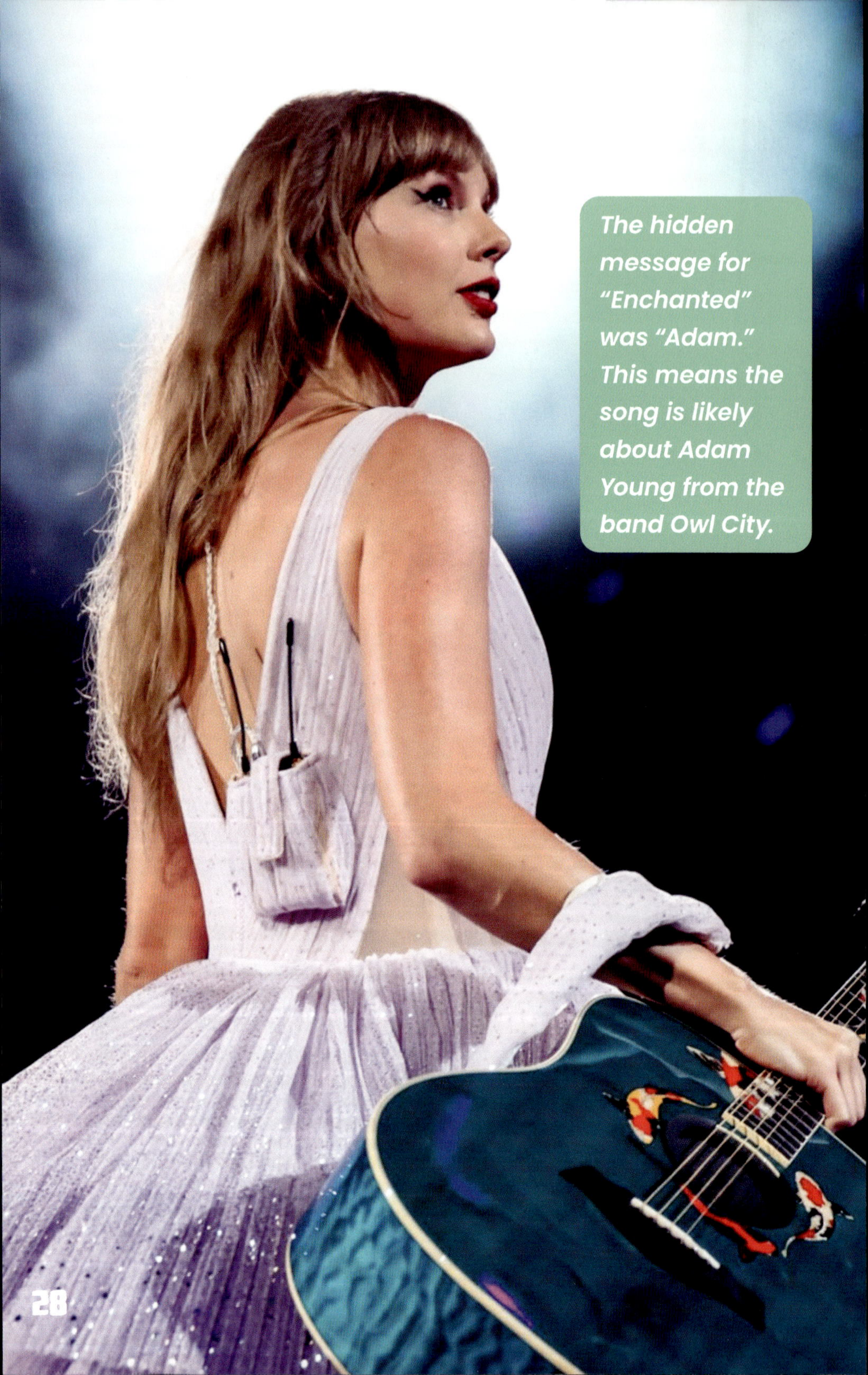

The hidden message for "Enchanted" was "Adam." This means the song is likely about Adam Young from the band Owl City.

During Taylor's Eras Tour, she originally included one song from *Speak Now*. After she finished her high-energy *Reputation* set, she came out in a gorgeous ball gown while the stage lit up with different hues of purple. Every night she sang "Enchanted." During some concerts, she also included "Long Live." These two songs were not originally **singles** from the album, but they were fan favorites.

MAKING CONNECTIONS

TEXT-TO-SELF

What is your favorite song from the *Speak Now* Era? Why is it your favorite?

TEXT-TO-TEXT

Have you read books about any other music artists? How are they similar to or different from Taylor Swift?

TEXT-TO-WORLD

As a reader, why do you think so many people around the world connect with Taylor Swift and her music? Write a few sentences to explain your answer.

GLOSSARY

anthem — an exciting song that is connected with a certain group or movement.

critic — a person whose job is to judge music, movies, plays, art, or literature. A critic critiques.

debut — to appear for the first time, or the first appearance.

direct — to lead and instruct in the making of a film, play, music video, etc.

Grammy — one of many yearly awards presented for remarkable work in music at the Grammys.

memorabilia — items with a special connection to a person or event.

produce — to organize the creation of music recordings. A person who produces is a producer.

single — a song that is released as a stand-alone from the album.

studio — a place where recordings are made.

INDEX

DiscoverRoo!

ONLINE RESOURCES

This book is filled with videos, puzzles, games, and more! Scan the QR codes* while you read, or visit the website below to make this book pop.

popbooksonline.com/SpeakNow

*Scanning QR codes requires a web-enabled smart device with a QR code reader app and a camera.